Nigger For Life

Joy Hamilton

Hearts to heart
minds to mind
Souls to Soul
 Oneness
United in our struggle
 to be free

Neal Hall MD

Copyright © 2009 by Neal E. Hall, M.D.

All rights reserved. No part of this book may be reproduced or transmitted in any form or by any means, electronic or mechanical, including photocopying, recording or by any information storage and retrieval system or stored in a data base without prior permission in writing from the publisher.

Info@NiggerForLifeBook.com
www.SurgeonPoet.com

ISBN 0-9729730-4-4
Manufactured in the United States of America.

First Edition

"I sense Dr. Hall's hypersensitivity to suffering-Martin, Malcolm and Jesus all had this same hypersensitivity. Both sides of his soul have prophetic leanings; his poetry has the capacity to change ordinary people's philosophy on social and racial issues. Like brother Malcolm, Dr. Hall is the activist who wants to change the world."

Cornel West, Ph.D.
Professor
Princeton University

Preface

Neal E. Hall M.D., Poet

Dr. Hall earned his undergraduate degree at Cornell University where he achieved All Ivy, All East Coast, and All American Honors. He Co-Captained The Cornell Track and Field Team and was named Cornell's Athlete of the Year. He was Gold Medalist in the '78 U.S. National Sport Festival Mini Olympics, was inducted into the Cornell University Athletic Hall of Fame and became an Inductee, Cornell University Quill and Dagger Senior Honorary Society.

He earned his Medical degree at Michigan State University and his ophthalmology surgical subspecialty training at Harvard University. He is now a physician and surgeon in private practice.

Dr. Hall presents the unfathomable dichotomy of eye surgeon and reactionary poet. The latter is where his anthology of poems lies waiting to bleed beneath white and black skins alike, to confront America, to shine the light of reason and rationality in its eyes.

In a *Nigger For Life*, Dr. Hall is able to capture his emergence from the sidelines of academia onto the exploitative and predatory playing fields of what he calls the "unspoken America." Here he discovered – painfully – that race has everything to do with choice, opportunity, power and freedom.

It's no ordinary muse that has Dr. Hall becoming as much a part of his poetry as his poetry has become a part of him. Rather it's a deep sense of betrayal combined with a passion for life that shows through in candid words and wrenching clarity. He can't help but bare his intelligence, his wit and his dreams. His anthology is as confronting as it is illuminating, as disarming as it is thought provoking.

Whether he works as an ophthalmologist or poet, his reality is clear-cut. In the eyes of "unspoken America," he is a *Nigger For Life*.

♠

Dedicated to
the fathers of my fathers,
as far back through slavery
to their lands of Africa.

♠

In Memory of
Mrs. Ethel Elaine Jackson
Sunrise: December 9, 1928
Sunset: May 29, 2009
Together, we were going to save the world.

Introduction

> *Christians speak of being born again.*
> *The Buddhist speaks of enlightenment.*
> *Not until I experienced*
> *the Zenist's satori,*
> *this sudden awakening,*
> *did I come to the realization that*
> *despite all accomplishments...*
> *despite all insurmountable obstacles*
> *faced and overcame,*
> *to white America,*
> *I am a Nigger For Life.*
>
> *Neal E. Hall, M.D.*

As a young boy, I was taught to believe Washington never told a lie, Lincoln freed the slaves, that the American dream was a reality well within the reach of every American. All I needed to do to make this dream mine was apply myself – self-motivation, discipline, hard work and education.

After 12 years of academic rigors, freshly minted from Harvard with a medical-surgical subspecialty (ophthalmology) in tow, I discovered painfully, that despite all my hard work, enthusiasm and drive, America does not deliver equally.

I discovered that in "unspoken America," race is the one thing on which I am "first" judged, by which I am "first" measured, "first" against which my life and accomplishments are metered diminished value, dignity and equality; all of which, have everything to do with accessing choice, opportunity, power and freedom.

In my quiet and pensive moments of introspect, I have found emancipation of mind in words poetically amassed and arranged in a *Nigger For Life*.

Now I can see, painfully disguised from the child I used to be, America's continued state of slavery.

There will be Whites who will criticize what will be described by them as the liberal and discriminating use and categorization of all White people in the phraseologies White people or White America.

Before such criticism is levied, let each White or wanna be White critic reveal when and how they have fully relinquished the color coded social, political and economic advantages their white or wanna be white skin affords them in White America.

At such point in time, will Whites have the right and standing to levy such criticism.

♠

How to Read this Anthology
Suggestion by the Author

Read the book sequentially – start at the beginning and work towards my final verse. The writings have spanned several years, commencing before 1990.

Many of my writings are intentionally without titles. These works take you to the essence of the poem without the prejudice of a header.

Titled works provide the reader clarity and direction. Often, the title was the inspirational flash which provoked the writing.

The table of contents lists both titled and untitled poems. Titled poems are in bold.

Please note the "spade" icon indicates the end of each poem.

♠

Table of Contents

1776 Declaration of Independence: 1st Draft[1]	1
Pretense and Pretext	3
For a totalitarian government[2]	4
In saying and doing nothing	5
Niggers are not born	6
Diallo	7
A Voice	8
Truth is	9
We either have no dreams	10
It	11
Even though	12
I am under no illusions	13
Love and hate are created equally	14
There is	15
It is life's contradictions tainted with hypocrisy	16
Drawn within the tautness	17
Civil Men Do	18
We are conduits of	19
First Served	20
Progress	21
In Black and White	22
The Point	23
Casting	24
The majority of White Americans	25
In art	26
Equal heights	27
Martin Luther King's birthday	28
Always Some	29
Black man's lips	30

---

[1] **Bold** is the poem title
[2] Non-bold is the first line of an untitled poem

Racial tension simmers	31
True Multiculturalism	32
Grass Roots	36
In front of you	37
Color	38
Be not deceived by people	39
In America	40
Liberty is a chalice few men hold	41
Politically speaking	42
We all are prostitutes of some sort	43
White Man Asked Me	44
No shore for refuge	45
There are those who lead men in prayer	46
Religion	47
The Greatest of These	48
In an attempt to protect ourselves	49
The Declaration and Constitution placed	50
Diversification	51
People love winning.	52
There is no evil	53
The world's natural course is weighted	54
Weeds and Hate	55
Profiling	56
We are	58
Father forgive them not	59
While we have been chasing	60
You can rise up	61
The Last of What's Left	62
Everybody is in bed with somebody	63
White people will only do right	64
Politicians can't get anything done	65
When black people do wrong	66
Follower	67
All in One	68

White righteousness is	69
Neutralize	70
Through institutionalized misinformation	71
White America wants me to believe	72
The black man wraps himself in a flag hoist	73
In the Land of	74
Sisters Say	76
Attitude, Aptitude, Altitude	77
Trying to be a black man in America	78
Racial injustice and intolerance	79
Standing	80
There are black people	81
Collateral Benefits	82
To provide for America's national interest	83
Are we not prisoners of ourselves	84
I'm a good little Negro	86
Some men see soaring birds	87
Purpose	88
Inner Light	89
Despite your expectations of me	90
It is the nature of humans	91
There is a truth	92
Because I see what eyes cannot see	93
No Faith in Faith	94
Great men say nothing	96
Are we humans	97
Need to be in a place	98
We don't have enough freedom	99
I've learned to what extent people will go	100
Hence Forward	101
A man can only have two masters	102
Overcoming the fear of	103
Paradox	104
Just when I believe I am about	106

White people ask for patience	107
When people are too outwardly loud	108
Becoming	109
Lie unmoved against me	110
Welcomed change must always pass	111
Great men change bad laws	112
Freedom and dignity are like	113
He that hears with his eyes…	114
Surrounding myself in isolation	115
Freedom is a limited commodity	116
Freedom Lost	117
We don't all need to be the same color	118
I have found within me that anger	119
We continue futile efforts to persuade	120
While I realize that we all cannot	121
Unto Moses, the purist of heart	122
Webster defines entrepreneurship	123
We are socialized and emotionalized	126
The evolution of freedom for all men	127
Freedom is determined in part by the	128
First and Foremost	129
If we would rely more on the experiences	130
True greatness	131
Better Served	132
Patronization	133
We must transform and transfix	134
The world would be better off if Jesus	135
What People Do	136
You People	137
I Don't Hang	138
Folks	140
Mohammad Ali	141
Benjamins	142
Life is not enough	143

I am not brave	144
In There	146
Marcus Garvey was not racist nor racism	147
There is always a ray	148
A kindling crowd is just a hang man's noose	149
I's Free	150
Nigger For Life	152
Outside Inside of Outside	154
Telltale Air	156
Friendly Mr. white man	157
By Reason of Blackness	158
Knowing What I Be Knowing	160
More Deception Than Reparation	162
Massa put brands on us to put discernable	164
Signature Blend	165
First to Die	166
We The People	167
I can give no more time	168
Prayer of Exodus	169
Article I, Section II	172
I've got to keep moving	174
Speaking In Black	176
The greatest force in life	177
Dr. Nigger	180
9-11, 24-7	182
Having been imprinted to what appeared to	186
Tuskegee Air Men	193
Straight Ahead	194
An effective black leader	195
White Snow	196
In everywhere I turn	198
When massa's whip grew to be	200
Slavery	203
A Nigger Can't Write a Manifesto	204

Between Soiled Sheets	208
Past	211
Give to Get	212
The Look of Freedom	214
With hair like wool and feet as black as burnt	216
Ray	219
N-Word	222
Six Letters Away	224
Citadel	226
Preoccupation with occupation…	228
Of Freedom	229
Choice?	231
Heralded Strategies	232
Hope and Rescue	234
This We Wear	235
Mottos of Hypocrisy	236
And God Said	238
Urban Slave Ships	240
It Don't Stop	241
Nigger Intelligencia	242
True Savior	243
Democracy	244
Footnote	245
Clockwise	246
Breakdown	247
Said If I	248
Been to the mountain top	250
High Mentality	252
Property	254
Like Mine	255
Epilogue	256
Index	259

Nigger For Life

Poetry is nearer to vital truth than history.

- Plato -

1776 Declaration of Independence: 1ˢᵗ Draft

WHEN, in the course of human events, it becomes necessary for *We The People* to assert that *We* are entitled to all the resources and powers of this New World and, to assume such, shall, contrary to the Laws of Nature and the Opinions of Mankind, dissolve ourselves of that which connects all men to one another.

WITH the assent of the governed and sanctity of divine providence, *We* declare these truths and these our causes which impel us to separate; compel us to segregate and to enslave those to be of lesser constitution.

AND, *We* hold these truths to be self-evident, that all men are not created equal; that We, the founding fathers and our descendants are an anointed few, endowed by the creator with certain unalienable rights; that among these are the right to usurp the lives, liberties and pursuits of happiness of those of Negroid descent.

AND, that to secure these rights, *We* will weave into the fabric and foundation of this newly conceived nation these tenets as a lasting means to consolidate and maintain exploitative powers in such a form as to us shall seem most likely to ensure our lives, our fortunes and our sacred honor and that of our descendants over Negroid descendants for generations to come.

Having moored an indelible tenor for our lasting prosperity, *We The People* can ferret no lucid wherefore to partition the spoils of our dominion and usurpations with the present King of Great Britain (George III) from whom *We,* now and unceasingly, declare our independence. [1]

♠

---

[1] Adaptation of the *1776 Declaration of Independence*

Pretense and Pretext

England makes plain
its sovereignty in
King and Queen,
Prince and Princess,
in Dukes, Duchesses and Earls
who make no pretense
of public reign and rule
over servant and subject.

America disguises her monarchs
in Presidents and Vice Presidents,
Senators and Congressmen,
in Governors, Mayors and Councilmen
who reign and rule under the pretext of
public servants.

♠

For a totalitarian government
to remain disguised
as democratic,
it must have as a prerequisite,
an inept and incompetent electorate.
How else could a majority
mistake corruption for democracy?
Unless, however, that majority
is more corrupt than inept,
more corrupt than incompetent.

♠

In saying and doing nothing
there is the deference of acquiescence
or defiance of noble resolve.

Saying and doing nothing is not the problem.

Saying and doing nothing, in any form,
for too much and too long is.

When you hunger eat.
When you itch scratch.
When you thirst drink.

When you see that you are not free,
you must say and do, to be free.

To say and do nothing in any form
for too much and too long is
the acquiescence of noble resolve.

To be free,
defiantly say and do
with noble resolve.

♠

Niggers are not born.

There is no innate genetic material
that multiplies and divides into a nigger.

There are however,
white advantages to be secured
and maintained in creating niggers
to keep them niggers.

Niggers are not born,
they are the self-serving fabrications
of white capitalists.

♠

Diallo

Like Albany...
Like Selma... like Montgomery,
like it was before they said
things had changed,
it's Lynchburg, Virginia all over again.

In a dimly lit corridor of racist white America,
a black man shot nineteen times reaching for
his wallet,
alleged to be a gun.

Like in Albany... like South Boston...
like Jackson, Mississippi,
like things never changed
even though they said things changed,
like Albany... like Birmingham all over again.

♠

A Voice

Without a voice,
without a cry,
how can I rise
above myself?
How can I live,
how can I not die,
without a voice,
without a cry?

♠

Truth is
the reflection
deep within our recesses
revealing the lies
upon which
we've built
our being.

♠

We either have no dreams
or linger too long in those we have.

♠

It

Because we fought so hard and
willingly died to hold It,
we cannot wake up to the realization
that It
is not freedom
but the tools to obtain It.

♠

Even though
we've been given more room
to roam about since the days of slavery,
the sign on the fence
that keeps us in our place
and defines the boundaries
of our life, liberty and pursuit of happiness
still reads plantation.

♠

I am under no illusions
that I am totally free,
ultimately in control
of life and destiny.

To believe otherwise,
leaves me vulnerable
to the lies of democracy.

♠

Love and hate are created equally,
strategically deployed like white and black chess pieces across a
checkered field of graded pawns;
divinities pondering their next moves.

Love and hate do not love and hate.
They seduce,
filling voids with signs and symbols.
They give hope and prospect which energizes
their immortal struggle,
adding drama to divine theaters.

Life was never ours to live.
So I stopped living there
on that checkered field.
I stopped trying to understand.
Stopped trying to find pleasure, measure,
and meaning in the next play.

To be free,
I don't love and I don't hate.
I just wait for deities
to ponder their next move.

♠

There is
no democracy,
only varying degrees
of tyranny.

♠

It is life's contradictions tainted with
hypocrisy that is the fundamental cause
of man's insanity.

Hope that would blossom eternal
dies before life's discrepancies.

Daily despair becomes too much to bear,
so insanity blurs the distinct edges of this
reality to some lesser truth we can bear.

♠

Drawn within the tautness
of the bow's caress,
freedom is an arrow bent,
to miss its stated mark.

♠

Civil Men Do

Inherently egocentric,
man is instinctively sinister.

Left to his own devices,
he will do malice and evil.

Humanity's necessity
for State and police
to secure civic order and peace
bears fair claim to
bad and evil civil men do,
left to their own doings.

♠

We are conduits of
greed,
exploitation,
poverty
and ignorance.

Without us, these matters
take no shape nor form,
know no time,
have no voice,
can find no stage
upon which to perform
their sufferings.

♠

First Served

Like the lion that eats before his pride,
political minds and royal lines
spew from forked tongues parsed words
spun into a spin from each
of the two faces from which they speak,
to serve first themselves
from the table of human resources.

♠

Progress

Today,
they don't call you Nigger.

Well !

not loud enough for you to hear.

♠

In Black and White

When America cries out for
a return to her days of greatness
memorialized in the still life in
Black and White photos,

When America yearns
to return to those days now proclaimed
to be her greatest hour of glory and honor,
of family values and morality,
of ten commandments,
of I am my brother's keeper,
of godliness and god-fearing,
of liberty and justice for all,

Remember, memorialized in
America's black and white still life,
there is no black life.

♠

The Point

There is always a point beyond which
Whites will not go.

Whites will push the envelope of
sounding Black,
dressing Black,
acting Black,
appearing to support Black,
having that one friend be Black.

Whites will do so, up to,
but not beyond the point they
become indistinguishable as being White,
thus forfeiting the ill-gotten cache of
rights, privileges and entitlements afforded
whites in a race-based discriminating society.

♠

Casting

The fathers of my father
did not sacrifice nor die
that I may gain the right to cast my vote
for the lesser of two evils.

The lesser of two evils is still evil.
Yet, the Black man is indoctrinated
with the lesser standard of casting his one vote
for the lesser of two evils;
as if the casting itself,
under any circumstance,
is more sacred than the right to not cast
one's vote for any greater or
lesser portion of evil.

♠

The majority of White Americans
will have you believe that it is
an isolated minority of Whites
responsible for the majority of racism
that minorities experience to the benefit
of the majority of White Americans.

♠

In art,

we look for and

create truth and virtue.

In life,

we avoid and destroy them.

♠

Equal heights,
unequal colors.

Ignorance and greed
keeps one man's head held higher;
another man's head lower
than the other.

♠

Martin Luther King's birthday
has been transformed into
a day of atonement.

The one day white America uses to absolve
itself of the previous 364 days of continuous
racial oppression, injustice and exploitation.

♠

Always Some

It is not always just black and white.
But, I have lived long enough as a Black man
to know that there is always some black and
always some white despite what they say.

♠

Black man's lips
became full holding back
for so long, words for
White man's injustice.

♠

Racial tension simmers
just above the surface
of white economics.

♠

True Multiculturalism

Throughout history
man has made his way and fortunes
dividing and subdividing mankind.

Dividing and subdividing is sine qua non for
conquering mankind. To conquer and maintain
that conquest, the conqueror must first
institutionalize exploitation of some
inextinguishable distinguishing attribute to pit
one part, one group against the other.

The institutionalization of exploitation
and the perpetuation of division keeps us in
continuous discord; distracted from discerning
and defying a ruling majority who segregates,
exploits and establishes social standing through
distinctions that are infinitesimally insignificant
and exponentially inextinguishable.

Wittingly and unwittingly,
in celebrating inextinguishable distinguishing
differences, the divided become accomplices,
systematically fractionalized and propagandized
to perpetuate impregnated inferiority and
discord in search of hollow superiority over their
fellow man.

Generation after generation we continue to create a sense of self greater than and separate from the whole.
A self divided and subdivided from its oneness. This, we are made to believe and celebrate as our individual culture.

Our greater-than-thou sense of a superior self and culture separated from its whole makes us consorts with those who would exploit it to keep us divided amongst ourselves, while they rob our divided house of its treasured oneness... of its life and liberty.

Our myopic view of multiculturalism sharpens our focus on our differences and subconsciously reinforces the notions that we are not the same, that we are not cast from the same die... from the same oneness.

Life linked to liberty linked to social standing linked to perceptional differences fosters distraction, distrust and discord.
It misdirects one's focus from one's true mission, our strength in being one.

And, therein lies the basis for our continued exploitation, continued second class citizenship... our continued conquest.

Our celebration of the conqueror's manipulated and exploitative multiculturalism has been and will continue to be used to divide our power of oneness into frictional diminishing fractions.

True multiculturalism should seek to have you find something within your perceived self, something within your perceived culture that connects and unites you to someone other than your perceived self; connects and unites you to some culture other than your perceived culture.

True multiculturalism should bring you to one point, to one place, to one culture, to one united house, whose men and women are all brothers and sisters despite the fact they call themselves Asians, Hispanics, Whites, Blacks or any other ethnic subtype.

The celebration of designations and distinctions laced with the venomous indoctrination to rise to the top of the bottom is weaponry of exploiters and exploitation.

It is the privateer's game of divide and conquer. If we are to prevail, it must not be the game we play. We must not be distracted from discerning and defying a ruling majority.

True multiculturalism brings you to one point, to one place, to one culture, to one house, united amongst itself.

♠

Grass Roots

We say grass roots,
but whose grass roots are we rooted?

Who's last when it comes to first?
Who's first to be last?

Whose ass do we cover,
whose do we pass when we discover
green in the grass?

We say grass roots
but they have not discovered...
... have yet to uncover
whose grass you are rooted.

♠

In front of you,
behind me, foot steps left
to step across the
quicksand of white justice
and injustice.

♠

Color

Color does
what colors do.
Color colors everything.

♠

Be not deceived by people
who would have you believe
power corrupts.

Power left to its own doings
is power,
no more, no less.

It is people
who are corrupt,
misusing power in their corruption
to perpetuate their corruption
to maintain power.

♠

In America,
my skin color is
the thorned crown about my head.

And with each blood tinged step I take,
I wipe the blood from my forehead
with the blood from the palms of my hands.

♠

Liberty is a chalice few men hold
and fewer still do they allow
to sip freely from it.

♠

Politically speaking,
there is
what politicians tell the public
and there is
the truth.

Politics is the politician
hiding truth from public view
as a means of ascending to
and retaining power
in public office.

♠

We all are prostitutes of some sort,
lying down, compromising
something of ourselves.

♠

White Man Asked Me

A White man asked me to
be less than a man so that he could
find a face-saving way out.

He asked me to help him
dishonor my wife that he might find
a face-saving way
to appear honorable before his.

A White man asked me to be
less in the eyes of my people
so that he could find a face-saving way
to appear to be more than he is
in the eyes of his people.

♠

No shore for refuge,
how do you keep truth afloat
in a wide open sea of lies?

♠

There are those who lead men in prayer
and those that lead men in battle
that all men may have the right to pray.

♠

Religion

God's devotion or
man's notion of how
to exploit his fellow man's need
to have an explanation
of the unexplainable
in order to comfort fears
of his unknowns.

♠

The Greatest of These

A rock
a club
a bow and arrow
a sword
a gun
a bomb
a canon
a tank
a plane
a bigger bomb
a guided missile
a misguided missile
and the greatest of these... religion,
that have taken the lives of men.

♠

In an attempt to protect ourselves,
we hide our true self behind some distant
contrived layered antithesis of ourselves.

What we reveal of self to keep concealed
is remote and contrary to who we really are.

♠

The Declaration and Constitution placed too much trust in founding fathers and not enough distrust of men entrusted to ensure that the Constitution had enough constitution;

that America's Declaration declared, with enough conviction, equally for all men.

♠

Diversification

Blacks view diversification to include
that which has been purposefully excluded
as a means to move toward equality.

To whites, it is the callous pursuit
of diversified streams of income commandeered
in colored inequities contrived to purposefully
exclude color from equal opportunity.

♠

People love winning.
It is the winner
they come to hate.

♠

There is no evil,
separate and distinct.

There is only man who calls it evil
to give himself
leave and distance
between what he is
and what he would have us believe
he is not.

♠

The world's natural course is weighted towards
disorder and destruction.
Since we are of this world,
this too is man's basic nature.

Throughout existence, man has tried to bring
order to this world and himself. In doing so, he
has strained and constrained disorder and
himself. In doing so, he has changed nature
and the nature of himself.

That which we expend to accomplish this is life.
But in time, the will and way of the world is too
great and unwilling.

In time, man is consumed by that
natural course of things. In time,
time bears witness that we are
no more than the natural course of things.

♠

Weeds and Hate

The world ain't right yet to plant seeds.
The fields are too full with weeds and hate;
no fertile ground left for love to grow.

Out of the south
the prevailing winds are hostile
heading north;
the world ain't right.

We have more fear than we do courage.
We don't live together,
we survive at the expense of one another.

Can't plant seeds in
fields too full with weeds and hate.
The world ain't right yet,
no fertile ground left to plant peace.

♠

Profiling

Profiling is a policy targeting specific individuals or groups of individuals possessing certain physical and cultural characteristics which would lead one to believe that said individuals or groups have a greater penchant to engage in unlawful acts.

Yet, we don't pull to the side of the road white upscale female realtors who have a greater propensity to engage in redlining black home buyers away from predominantly white neighborhoods.

We don't pull to the side of the road gun toting southern white males driving gun racked confederate flagged pick up trucks who have a greater propensity to engage in hate crimes against blacks.

We don't pull to the side of the road distinguished looking middle-aged white male doctors who have a greater propensity to engage in racial biases in the delivery of health care to African Americans.

We don't pull to the side of the road three-pieced suspendered white male bankers who have a greater propensity to engage in predatory lending and disproportionately denying loans to Blacks.

We don't pull to the side of the road white politicians who have a greater propensity to engage in activities to sell our lives, liberty and pursuit of happiness.

Profiling in its truest sense is no more than white racism, discrimination, exploitation and hypocrisy shrouded in self-serving plausible deniability.

♠

We are
no different from early man.

We still live in villages separated by our fears.

We still lay siege upon one another
because of our fears of one another.

We are
still savages despite the pretense of civility.

♠

Father forgive them not
for they know what they do.

Their conspiracies unseen,
hidden deep within
their plausible deniabilities.

Father forgive them not
for they know what they do.

♠

While we have been chasing dreams of liberty,
America has conveniently forgotten that
it was born out of the same tyranny
it now metes out to people of color.

♠

You can rise up
beyond the hood,
but massa will never let you
leave his plantation.

♠

The Last of What's Left

I am what's left of
the screams of cracked parched lips,
of backs bent back with
the crack of the white man's whip.
I am the last of what's left.

I am the last of faceless, melanous,
shadowed figures bent forward,
slumping amidst the musket's dispersing
cloud of copious smoke.

I am what's left of the last.
I am the last of what's left.

I am the last of plantations and reservations, of
urban displacement and economic exploitation.

I am what's left of gentrification,
of race-based discrimination and deprivation,
of what whites left
of the screams of cracked parched lips
and backs bent back.

I am what's left of the last.
I am the last of what's left.

♠

Everybody is in bed with somebody.
We all sleep in somebody else's bed.
We all have a price.
We all pay some asking price.
We all have a bed waiting somewhere
to compromise ourselves.

♠

White people will only do right
when they have a clear advantage
and that advantage has been institutionalized
and socialized to remain in their clear favor to
the extent that when they are forced to do right,
it will have no bearing on a fair and equitable
outcome for all God's creations.

♠

Politicians can't get anything done because
they don't hold each other accountable for
anything because
they all know that they're all guilty
of doing something.

♠

When black people do wrong,
white people want justice.
When white people do wrong,
white people want closure, healing
and to get on about the nation's business.

♠

Follower

We are so preoccupied with following,
we can't lead nor be lead away from those
who would have us just follow.

♠

All in One

With repeated deference to the doctrine
of reasonable doubt, white inequities and
injuries are discretely packaged and centrifuged
into transgressions of an isolated few.

Yet, America is quick to stylize and televise
all black people to the fears of all white people
in the transgression of one black person.

♠

White righteousness is worn
like genteel fleece concealing
the ravenous wolf beneath.

White America has mastered the art of
disguising savage aggression and usurpation
beneath plausible deniability and
the pretense of civility.

♠

Neutralize

In the practice of tai chi, there is a play fighting exercise - push hands.

One of the major objectives of this exercise is to neutralize first that force emanating from your opponent of greatest threat to you.

And so, on a continuum, whites neutralized Garvey, then Dubois, then Malcolm, then Martin, all in an unceasing effort to further contain and neutralize us.

♠

Through institutionalized misinformation and miseducation, we have been brainwashed, filled with self-hate and doubt.

We have been trained to be more adept at looking after the properties and interests of the white man then at acquiring and securing our own properties and interests.

We have come to view subservience to massa's cause as evidence of upward mobility, success and emancipation.

♠

White America wants me to believe
the wheels of justice turn slowly intrinsically,
detained by deference to uncolored
judiciousness.

But in the lay of this land, uncolored
judiciousness does not exist. True justice is
precluded from turning in and of itself.

White hands detain judicial spin long enough
to spin fast enough to give false hope, yet
slow enough to secure in their grasp
economic and institutional advantages over
black America, long before justice is allowed
to turn uncolored.

♠

The black man wraps himself in a flag, hoist
half-mast high enough by white America
to fully wrap itself in, to justify usurping
the black man.

♠

In the Land of

In the land of Washington and Jefferson,
there have always been Talibans.

There have always been sleeper cells
hidden behind the ideas and ideals of
a fabricated America...

behind democrats and republicans,
behind one man and one vote,
behind a hollowed statue of Liberty and
the appearance of balanced scales of justice.

In the land of Jackson and Madison,
there have always been Talibans,

sleeper cells woven into the fabric of
51 stars and 13 red and white stripes,

sleeper cells hidden from the light of day
and behind white sheets that ride in
the black of night.

In the land of Hopkins and Franklin,
there have always been Talibans,

white Americans, waging an economic
Jehad of terror against people of color.

In the land of Nixon and Clinton,
there have always been Talibans,
white Americans, asleep behind the
ideas and ideals of "one nation under God
indivisible with liberty and justice for all." [1]

♠

---
[1] The Pledge of Allegiance by Francis Bellamy, 1892.

Sisters Say

Adorned in self-proclaimed
African sounding names,
Sisters say they want to be like the motherland;
wear their hair like Africa,
happily and naturally,
Afrocentric, without the nappy.

Purchased, permed and braided with
body and bounce,
Sisters say they want to be like the motherland.

Want to wear African hair at the length of
Euro-hair; long, extending down past across
their asses to complement their aqua colored
contact lenses.

Flipped back, flung and swung to one side,
Sisters want to extend Africa from their heads,
want to pull it back and wrap their purchased
permed braids into wanna be blond pony tails
without the nappy.

Accessorized in blue colored contact lenses,
colored girls say they want to be
colored like the motherland;
wear their hair like Africa... colonized.

♠

Attitude, Aptitude, Altitude

Attitude without aptitude...

False prophets speaking in hip-hop tongues
leading the multitude
to red seas that do not part.

Aptitude without altitude...

Erudite middle class,
feeble with false pretense
and compromised convictions.

Judases,
unwilling to reach above their laurel crowns to
lead the multitude beyond the reach
of the task master.

♠

Trying to be a black man in America
is like freedom's thirst trying to
clench water within broken hands.

♠

Racial injustice and intolerance
starts at the top of political tickets
and trickles all the way down
to the assassin's trigger finger.

♠

Standing

It be not freedom,
but a distant thunder
that has yet to be fully heard or felt.

Its rumbling is not freedom,
it is the coming of freedom.

It be not freedom,
but a distant flash of light that pushes back the
night for but a brief second.
Its light is not freedom,
it is the coming of freedom.

It be not freedom,
but black men who over hundreds of years
have managed to crawl to their feet, yet
their backs remain bent,
their heads bowed,
their hearts burdened,
under the pressing weight
of race-based injustice.

Standing is not freedom,
it is the coming of freedom.

♠

There are black people
who are
too black,
too poor
and too powerless.

And there are blacks
who are too white to know
that white America believes them to be
too black,
too poor
and too powerless.

♠

Collateral Benefits

There are white folks
who boldly stand knee-deep
in negro killing fields,
discriminating, plundering,
taking, denying, segregating, killing.

And, there are white folks
who stand self-righteously
on the sidelines of those killing fields,
quietly doing, saying nothing to stay
the killings whilst reaping the social and
economic collateral benefits of ethnic genocide
by bolder white folks stacking black souls
knee-deep in negro killing fields.

♠

To provide for America's national interest and security, America has armed guards at its airports, train stations, bus stations and the Home Depots in black communities.

♠

Are we not prisoners of ourselves,
timidly tiptoeing where others walk firmly;
our comings and goings leaving shallow
impressions, ensuring only our
comings and our goings?

We are not free men,
we have pseudo-liberty imposed by
self-imprisoned thoughts,
fearful of transformation into words of protest.

We are not free men, but
servants to the free flowing thoughts and
desires of others who boldly think and speak
beyond their appointed place and time.

We are status quo simmering in
a sea of stagnation.

We've become masters of a way without the will,
a mistress to submission;
eyes that will not see beyond white man's
vision, a silent voice that only listens.

Will we ever come to say,
when faced clearly with
the wrong and right of our day,
that we shall stand firmly in a righteous way
and compromise nothing of ourselves
but compromise itself?

♠

I'm a good little Negro
if I lay down and
let them put chains on me.

But, I'm a threatening
Nigger if I stand up
and fight to be free.

♠

Some men see soaring birds
and fly they too into
their dreams of yonder,
creating their own destiny
through the vividness of their thoughts,
the purity of their wisdom
and the conviction embedded
within their hearts.
Many of us have dreams,
few are those who make them reality.

♠

Purpose

It is not the life in living
that gives peace of mind to our existence.
The key to all men's sanity
lies in the purpose of their being.

♠

Inner Light

Our lives must shine
so that others traveling the same road of
hopes and desires may see their way through
the pain, success and adversity of life.

♠

Despite your expectations of me,
I will be what I shall be.

I may not arrive when you want me to,
but your time is not key when I shall be.

I may not arrive how you want me to.
The mode of my travel will be chosen by me.

Your choice has no bearing on this destiny.
I shall be despite your expectations of me.

I may not be where you want me to be
yet, wherever you find me, I shall be me.

I will not be what you want me to be
I shall be what I want me to,
if I am to be me.

♠

It is the nature of humans
to have 99% of all that they need
yet define themselves
by that 1% they cannot possess.

♠

There is a truth
I must define.

A truth,
I must find.

Left to others, it
will become their lie.

♠

Because I see what eyes cannot see,
Because I hear what others will not,
Because I walk where others dare not,
I will always stand alone.

♠

No Faith in Faith

Faith is the substance of
conquest and dependence on fixes
that rob men of their capacity to think
rationally and objectively about
and beyond their circumstances.

Faith is the substance of abuse,
infused into the piercing points of
views of patriotism and religion;
thrust like the pusher's needle
into the vessel of man
for submissive unresponsiveness to
systems of beliefs and ideals
that rob men of their capacity to think
rationally and objectively about
and beyond their circumstances.

Faith demands that we not question nor wonder;
that we acquiesce to blind obedience to
allegiance and holiness without dialogue or
debate; without learnt persuasion or reverence
to life's experiences.

Faith demands that we relinquish, as a sign of
our faith, civil liberties and a tenth of our
earnings to pious draped intermediaries who
hold themselves out to possess greater
experience in matters of utmost faith.

I am not a man of faith.
I have no faith in faith
that demands I have faith.

I have no faith in faith that
demands submissive unresponsiveness
to dominance.

I am the learned lessons, not of blind faith,
but the insightful revelations of my life's
experiences which ask no demands nor
recompense to establish beliefs and ideals in
me that build and enhance my capacity to
think rationally and objectively
about and beyond my circumstances.

I have no faith in faith
that diminishes my capacity to think
rationally and objectively.

♠

Great men say nothing
as the world listens with intent
to their actions.

♠

Are we humans
seeking a spiritual experience
or spirits in search of
a human existence.

♠

Need to be in a place
where I can safely place
my insides outside.

♠

We don't have enough freedom

to be free,

we have just enough,

to free ourselves.

♠

I've learned to what extent people will go
to get what you have and
to what extent I must go
to keep what I got.

♠

Hence Forward

Freedom,

if I caress you too much,
it's because I've never felt anything this soft.

If I hold you too tightly
it's because now that I am close to you,
I am too afraid to lose you.

If I move too fast,
it's because I have waited too long
to have you.

If I move too slowly,
it's because I must learn to walk
with unfettered feet.

If I should close my eyes,
weary and wanting for one brief moment,
it's because the road from whence I've come
seemed unending.

And, the road hence forward
is one I must travel
because it does not bind me to
one place or to anyone anymore
from hence forward.

♠

A man can only have two masters;
one his creator, one himself...
one he must serve, one he must conquer.

Have he any others,
he will surely fail at the first two.

♠

Overcoming the fear of
overcoming one's perceived limitations
is the dawn of one's greatness.

♠

Paradox

Wishing not to wish,
wanting not to want,
inescapable ironic contradictions.

Which is the greater sin,
wishing or wanting not to wish,
wanting or wishing not to want.

Never wanting the want
I take no leap of faith.
I make no moment mine to possess.
I can hold no water in the want
of wishing hands.

I cannot quiet sound nor
blow against the wind.
I cannot push back a sunrise nor
stop the night from falling.
I cannot pull back my bow and point my
arrow and hit love while simultaneously
missing sorrow.

While wishing or wanting not to wish,
wanting or wanting not to want,
I stand shapeless, weightless
amidst the dim mist of want and wish.

I can take no leap of faith.
I can make no moment mine to possess.
I can hold no water in the wish
of my wanting hands.

♠

Just when I believe I am about
to hit rock bottom,
I am somehow held from touching bottom's last;
brought back to some higher height
from which to rise again.

♠

White people ask for patience and
time to delay doing now, that
which they know is right.

It does not take time,
it takes people willing to do
the right thing right now.

♠

When people are too outwardly loud and assured, it's because they are overcompensating for a perceived inner weakness.

True confidence seeks not words nor demands a stage on which to speak them.

♠

Becoming

There is something uniquely special
turning inward within yourself
to perceive yourself watching yourself move;

to feel yourself growing, knowing,
becoming increasingly aware
of being aware of becoming yourself.

♠

Lie unmoved against me
my unsheathed skin,
this cold blade
singled, sharply edged,
tempered and poison tipped.

This cold blade made
more black than black should be,
more black than black can be,
turned against me to
cut deep in me,
lie against me unmoved.

Lie against me,
shield me in rebellion of black
made blacker than black should be,
blacker than black can be.

Endow me might of way
to turn thine tempered rage
blade side out to cut
outwardly more times than not,
this venomous fate
foul men doest plot.

♠

Welcomed change must always pass
through the unwanted hands
of status quo.

♠

Great men change bad laws.
Lesser men accept them.
Unscrupulous men hide behind them.

♠

Freedom and dignity are like
inhaling and exhaling.

You cannot have one
without the other.

You cannot choose one
over the other.

To live
you need both.

♠

He that hears with his eyes...
sees with his ears...
will come to learn that
truth is reality distorted.

It is a tale told by the oppressor
to perpetuate the oppression.

♠

Surrounding myself in isolation
with words spun into thought,
I emerge transformed,
a mind freed to be free.

♠

Freedom is a limited commodity demanding its price to obtain and sustain it.

The measure of one's freedom is directly proportionate to the amount of economics one has to obtain and sustain it.

♠

Freedom Lost

When I say that I am
and I am not,

When I dream I am
and a dream it remains,
that's freedom lost.

When I fail to plant
the seeds of my discontent
within the futile and fervent grounds
of my discontent,

When I fail to grow roots to hold steadfast
trees whose branches bear the fruit of my
liberty, that's freedom lost.

Every mind left closed,
Every day delayed,
Every minute missed,
Every way not made,
these chains remain...
that's freedom lost.

♠

We don't all need to be the same color.

What we need is a more equitable distribution of opportunities to obtain wealth.

♠

I have found within me that anger,
enough anger, that my focus
has been sharpened,
my resolve strengthen that I am
called to arms and action in this cause,
to its rightful end.

♠

We continue futile efforts to persuade white America to be empathetic, sympathetic and morally responsible for their contribution to the ongoing plight of black America.

Whites have neither the life experiences nor the economic incentive to do so.

We cannot create in them the life experiences, but we can and
we must create for them
the economic incentives to do so.

♠

While I realize that we all cannot
rise to the mountain's top,
there is however, some higher ground
greater than that which we currently find
ourselves standing upon, that
we can step up to.

♠

Unto Moses, the purist of heart, God
gave a *staff*, not to exalt himself,
not to glorify himself,
not to place himself above and apart from the
cries of bondage, but as an instrument through
which God would work his miracles to free men
from their pharaoh.

For black Americans,
economics is the *staff* given unto us
through which God will work his miracles.

I am certain the *staff* was given unto us.
I fear we cannot find among us,
a Moses pure of heart.

♠

Webster defines entrepreneurship or more specifically (entrepreneur) as one who organizes, manages and assumes the risk of a business or enterprise. Black Americans must think about this definition in the context of their struggle for freedom and equality in white racist America. The concept of entrepreneurship falls short of the real message we should hear and aspire to.

The real message is not entrepreneurship. It is ownership. Ownership is defined by *Webster* as having power over; to control, to be independent of assistance. It is this concept that is far more crucial to African Americans obtaining a meaningful measure of freedom and equality than the concept of entrepreneurship.

Raymond St. Jacques (a famous African American actor) said "The fundamental difference regarding the attitude White people have about acquiring wealth and the attitude Black people have is that White people know that wealth brings power, so they do everything possible to gain more wealth and thus more power.

Black people, too often, seek wealth to have enjoyment, to buy pleasure. There's a big difference between power and pleasure, and since power lasts longer than pleasure, Whites have gained control of practically everything."

Our message and focus should be ownership not entrepreneurship; leverage, but leverage not just for the sake of leverage, but leverage to empower us to make good, for all men, the freedoms, liberties and opportunities proffered in America's constitution.

The challenge we face, individually and collectively, is to utilize all our educational, civil and voting rights and opportunities to obtain that economic leverage to make good the promises of freedom in America for all people.

We are the hopes and dreams of nameless, faceless black slaves whose souls have yet to find a resting place for their suffering and their indignities.

As such, we are obligated and we must: (i) learn to develop strategies to minimize racist perceptions and presumptions until we are in a position of power to eradicate those perceptions and presumptions, (ii) seek ownership of responsible businesses that will provide us wealth and leverage for self-reliance, self-determination and self-governance and (iii) never allow ourselves to be lured into a false sense of security and acceptance in America.

♠

We are socialized and emotionalized to see our plight in black and white.

To do so, distracts from our economic truths.

This is not about black and white.

Its about resources and man's inability to live in harmony in a world where he perceives there to be a limited source of valued resources to control his destiny.

Our plight is in shades of green. Our struggle is that which it has always been from the time of our enslavement - the struggle to collectively acquire enough resources to leverage sustainable freedoms.

♠

The evolution of freedom for all men
white, black, brown, red or yellow
is deeply rooted in the sacrifices
the preceding generations made to advance
the economic standing of
the succeeding generation.

♠

Freedom is determined in part by the
oppressor and in part by the oppressed.

We can no longer allow ourselves
to be divided into black field slaves
and high yellow house niggers.

We must move from an economy of
consumers to an economy of producers.

We cannot continue to buy into
and live white America's notion of
how blacks should give back,
how we should discipline ourselves,
the tone and tenor of our mentors and heroes.

We must realize that we cannot save
everyone and that everyone does not
know how nor desire to be saved.

We must focus more of our limited
resources on the multitudes of Ten,
charging them to build the social, moral and
economic infrastructures that motivated
individuals among us can come to, to save
themselves and our people.

♠

First and Foremost

White people will always perceive
us as niggers first and foremost.

Though we may like to think otherwise,
their perception will remain our reality
until we develop self-sustaining,
self-determining economic infrastructures
that forever alter whites' self-serving
distortion of reality.

♠

If we would rely more on the experiences
God gives us rather than the faith man sells us,
each of us could remain free of mind and spirit
to contribute the full measure of ourselves to
the dialogue and discord that determines the
world's course.

I am not a man of faith.
I am a man of experience.
I don't capitulate to faith at
the expense of my experience.

♠

True greatness
is rooted in and grows from
the deepest depth of despair.

♠

Better Served

White people would have black people
believe we would be better served
as idealist and liberalist.

The reality of white racism reveals
that blacks would better serve themselves
as realist and capitalist.

♠

Patronization

White people will continuously shit on you everyday for free.

So why should blacks suffer further indignities by paying whites to do so.

♠

We must transform and transfix
free at last[1]
into freedom that lasts,
freedom that outlasts
one black generation
to the next black generation.

♠

---

[1] *American Negro Songs and Spirituals* by J.W. Work, 1940.

The world would be better off if Jesus
died to rid man of sinning rather than
forgive man for his sins.

To forgive mankind's sins
and not end mankind's sinning
has been the greatest sin against mankind.

♠

What People Do

People don't do big and important things.
People do things for
big and important people.

♠

You People

A nigga knows
when white people say
- you people, -

A nigga knows
that - you people - mean niggers,
thinly veiled in a sheered white hooded sheet;
shrewdly shrouding the bigot.

But, a nigga knows.

A nigga knows
what white people say
when white people say,
- you people. -

♠

I Don't Hang

From monkey to neanderthal,
from slave to slave wages,
from no seat to the back seat,
from none prior, to the first
and only colored they let through.

We did not deal this hand
so why are we playing these cards?

We are too content having our freedom
confined to whites granting us the right
to shit on the same toilet they shit on...

... to drink their spit from
the same fountain spigot they spit on...

... to eat their shit from the same counter
they sit and eat from.

I've come down from a different tree.
I don't hang and I don't swing.
I walk upright refusing to be content
with progressing from monkey to Neanderthal,

from slave to slave wages,
from no seat to the back seat,
from none prior, to the first
and only colored they let through to
shit on the same toilet they shit on,
to drink their spit and
eat from the same counter
they sit and eat from.

I've come down from a different tree.
I don't hang and I don't swing.
I walk upright.

♠

Folks

There are two Americas.

One created by enslaved black folks
for the benefit of white folks.

The other, created for enslaved black folks
by white folks, for the benefit of white folks.

♠

Mohammad Ali

Only when white America has exhausted all
legal and illegal means
to break your spirit and fight,
and you remain standing
uncompromised... then
will they de-nail you from their crucifix,
cut you down from the hang man's tree,
untie you from the whipping weeping willow
and call you a national hero,
a role model,
their national treasure.

♠

Benjamins

Whites will make you believe
it's duty, honor and service to
country and country men.
But to them, it's about the Benjamins.

Whites will tell you it's
about morals and morality,
freedom and equality.
But from beginning to end,
for them,
it's always about the Benjamins.

♠

Life is not enough
if you are not free enough
to live it.

♠

I am not brave.
I have not the options
to choose to be or not be;
to do or not do.
I've been thrown overboard
into an endless riptide.

I am a negro in America's undertows,
floundering beneath its surface.
I have no viable options against
nigger undersets and crosscurrents.

I have not the options
to choose to be or not be;
to do or not do.
I am black... I must be black.
I must stay black to be kept back.

Thrown overboard,
they usurped my to be or not to be;
my to do or not to do.

I am not brave.
I have not the options
to choose to be or not be;
to do or not do.

I've been thrown overboard
to tread neck high above
the surface of raging white waters.

I am not brave,
I am just treading in black.

♠

In There

It's in there.
It's always in there
when *whites* say:

Hey dude... nigger
Bro... nigger
Yo Bro... nigger

Cuz... nigger

Soul brother... nigger

My man... nigger
My main man... nigger
Whassup my main man... nigger

When Boss says boss, boss means nigger.

It's always there.
It's always in there.

When whites say how articulate and
intelligent you are, they're saying
my bad boss,
I thought you were a nigger.

♠

Marcus Garvey was not racist nor racism,
he was a reaction to racism.

W.E.B. Dubois was not racist nor racism,
he was a reaction to racism.

Malcom X was not racist nor racism,
he was a reaction to racism

Farrakhan is not racist nor racism,
he is a reaction to racism.
.
Mandela is not racist nor racism,
he is a reaction to racism.

Martin was not racist nor racism,
but, he was, for the white man,
the most palatable reaction to racism.

We can no longer afford to be palatable nor singled out as the most palatable in our reaction to racism or the racist.

We must be one in action in our reaction to racism and the racist.

♠

There is always a ray
of inextinguishable hope
to guide us through our
darkest hour of despair.

♠

A kindling crowd is just a hang man's noose
away from igniting into
a fiery mob against you.

People alleging to be your friends are easily
hustled and stirred into
a combustible crowd against you.

♠

I's Free

I's not Lizzie no mo,
a slave's name from slave holders.

I's free.
I's a new me.

Gots no mo time
to give massa's cotton fields.
I's free.
Gots my own field
of dreams to tend to.
I's not Lizzie no mo.

I's flying,
Gots my own sets of wings.
I's free.
Massa can't put no mo
claims and chains on me.
Gots my own com'ins and go'ins,
my don'ts and do'ins.

I's free.
I's a new me.

No mo time to give to massa's killing fields,
I's free.

Gots my own field of dreams to tend to.
I's not Lizzie.

I's not Lizzie no mo,
that slave's name from slave owners.

I's free.
I's name Free.

♠

Nigger For Life

When the white man needs
a place to place his blame,

When he needs
a fall guy to scorn and fall upon,

when he needs
a name to hide culpability behind,

a name to call to misdirect and disconnect his
madness from his methods of ill-conceived gain,

I am the named Nigger he calls.

I am the designated Nigger kept in my place to
misplace white blame and bear white shame.

I am the circle designee, cornered within the
four corners of a circular room, spun to spin in
one place to misplace white
accountability and liability.

I am the named Nigger kept on my knees
to ensure the white man and his history
parries the cost of my holocaust.

A Nigger for life,
I am the Nigger designee
the white man can't afford to set free
when he needs a lifetime of Niggers kept
in one place to call on to fall upon
to misdirect and disconnect his madness
from his methods of ill-conceived gains.

♠

Outside Inside of Outside

White degrees do not free black minds.
In four years time white degrees transform
black faculties into no more than graduated
quarries for American bred bipartisan apartheid.

When we are taught to read like the white man
sees things, white degrees will not set nor let us
free. They merely sashay us, one seat up from
the rear of separate and unequal buses
transporting us further to the outside of the
inside of outside.

When we are taught to write brittle and broken
words of freedom scribed and subscribed to by
self-serving hands of the white man, white
degrees don't set nor let us free. They temper
our mindful demur of subjugation with the
illusion of parity and the false prophesy of an
intrinsic right to the white man's self-declared
inalienable birthrights.

When we are deceitfully taught to think and
speak of securing an educational degree as if it
were the magic white key that suddenly turns off
black inequities, poverty and slavery; white
degrees do not free black minds nor do they free
black hands, black arms and black feet.

White degrees shackle our unsuspecting black faculties by ceremoniously infusing in tasseled caps and pleated gowns, the cunning conceit, that in fours years time, we are free.

When in reality black caps and black gowns cover from our greenless view, white chains that continue to bind us to false prophesies and illusions of parity, shrewdly fashioned in a kinder, gentler slavery devised to advance us further to the outside of the inside of outside.

♠

Telltale Air

When in the presence of blacks folks,
white folks ooze from open wounds
an aromatic stench of entitlement.

They stand taller,
they look further down and past us
to make clear their sense of dominance.

There is a telltale air of arrogance
which lays heavy on black skin like humidity;
draining me…weighing on me… stifling me to
make clear my slavery.

♠

Friendly Mr. white man, you
can pretend to be my brother man.

You can pretend to sympathize and empathize.

You may even muster enough within yourself
to reach outside your selfishness to ease my
protest.

But, you can never know the dark places I persist,
at the hands of you,

my friendly Mr. white man.

♠

By Reason of Blackness

As a black man, I place no faith in America's judicial system of institutionalized race-based culpability and criminality.

I am unstrung by a judicial system that permutes truth into a preponderance of contrived color coded circumstantial evidence to circumvent a black man's due process and true innocence.

I am undone by the presumption of guilt by reason of blackness until proven otherwise beyond an unreasonable and certain prejudicial doubt.

As a black man, I am unmanned with America's jurisprudence of separate and unequal justice cloaked as a thinly veiled mistress bearing scales of weights equally balanced with empty promises.

I am undone, judged by a group not of my peers nor of my life experiences.

I am unnerved by the enormous burden of proof put on me to evidence my innocence in a judicial system where my guilt has been institutionalized by reason of blackness.

♠

Knowing What I Be Knowing

Knowing what I be knowing now,
Who would I be?

Hearing what I be hearing not be
what they be really saying when
they say I be free,

Who would I be,
Malcolm or Martin?

Seeing now how free I really be
when I thought I be really free by now,

Who would I be,
Malcolm or Martin?

Standing now where I be now,
my feet not feeling freedom's ground.

Who would I be,
Malcolm or Martin?

Knowing what I be knowing now,
hearing what I be hearing, not be,

Seeing now how free I really be
standing now where I be standing not be free.

Dreaming freedom's possibilities or
framing, by any means necessary[1],
my freedom's outcome,

Who would I be, Martin or Malcolm?

Knowing now what I be knowing,
I would be Malcolm.

♠

---
[1] *By Any Means Necessary* Speech, June 1964, Malcolm X

More Deception Than Reparation

Civil rights is to human rights
what negro is to nigger,
more deception than reparation.

Conceived as a mitigator,
civil rights was a lesser concession
guilefully devised to disguise and misprize
the greater injustice and atrocities
white men have committed against humanity.

More deception than restoration,
civil rights allowed white America to fraudulently
appear redemptive and reparative to elude the
world's stage of human rights abusers.

More deception than remuneration,
civil rights allowed white America to retain
its concocted worldwide moral authority and
colonizing imposition while at the same time,
maintaining a predatory grip over black
Americans; albeit a lesser grip for appearance
sake.

More duplicity than indemnity,
civil rights is to human rights
what negro is to nigger...
more concession than redemption...
more deception than reparation.

♠

Massa put brands on us to put discernable
marks of face value on us
to segregate us and pit us against us.

Thin lips against full lips,
hazel eyes against brown eyes,
the miseducated against the uneducated,
to segregate us.

Good hair against bad hair,
yellow skin against brown against
black skin, to pit us against us.

From field niggers to house negroes,
massa put brands on us to put
discernable marks of face value on us,
to segregate us and pit us against us.

♠

Signature Blend

Nigger, Nigga, and Negro, three
distinct flavors of fabricated chocolates.

Dark, brown and wanna be white,
hollowed and infused with light
vanilla fudge to suit white America's
insatiable appetence for tempered
chocolates.

Nigger, Nigga, and Negro,
distinct signature blends,
uniquely home grown.

Dark, brown and wanna be whiter,
packaged and sold as chocolate covered
niggers, segregated and individually
preserved, wrapped tightly
in stars and stripes forever.

♠

First to Die

If Martin inspired souls,
Malcolm fed them.

If Martin could bend,
Malcolm would not break.

If Martin was our brightest light,
Malcolm was the door that led
the way and day out.

There were no ifs, ands, nor buts
about Malcolm.

That is why he had to be the first to die.

February twenty first, nineteen sixty five.

♠

We The People

You can't get and
you won't find black people in
We The People

because

America won't let and
America don't let black people in
We The People.

♠

I can give no more time
to the future of things;
that which is not.

I have given enough time
to the past;
that which was.

I have only time
for here and now;
that which infinitely is.

♠

Prayer of Exodus

If thou be God, O God,
hear this my plea.

We are but a people, not unlike
the twelve descendants of Jacob's loins,
set over unto taskmasters.

We are estranged strangers in a strange land,
afflicted with bitter burden and brutal bondage.

We have toiled for too long
in all manners of servitude in America's
fields and treasured cities.

Have you not heard our cries
by reason of our taskmaster?

If thou be God, O God,
are we not chosen amongst the chosen ones?

Have you turned from us?

We have no Moses to lead us.
Slaughtered or jailed, we have no male child
to place upon the Nile in an ark of bulrush
to deliver us.

But, if thou be God, O God,
hear this my plea.

Though, I am but a pilgrim whose unholy
feet are set hereto in barren land.
A pilgrim, not of the Levi house,
whose weak hands have not
the strength to break the bonds that
bind us the fate of Jacob's loins.

Guide me O thou great Jehovah,
pilgrim through this barren land.
I am weak but thou art mighty.
Hold me with thy powerful hand.[1]

Put off my shoes from off my feet that
I may stand before your eternal flame
to be made fit and worthy.

In my hollow words place
thine immeasurable will and way
that the cries of my people
may be delivered from this barren land
across dry ground through parted sea unto
the land flowing with peace and prosperity.

If thou be God, O God
hear this my prayer.[2]

♠

---
[1] Guide me O Thou Great Jehovah, Hymn: William Williams 1745; New adaptation by John or William Williams 1772
[2] Author's adaptations of Exodus Chapter 1: 5,11,13; Chapter 3: 3, 23-25; Chapter 3: 5,7-8; Chapter 33: 3

Article I, Section II

Three-fifths[1] of five-fifths,
the white man said
as if he were the creator of all things.
I was two-fifths too short a human being.

To mitigate taxation to
further cash reserves, the slave master,
as if he were the creator of all things,
constitutionalized my fractionalized
representation when he wrote
in his constitution:

two-fifths too short a human being.

Two arms, two hands, two-fifths too short,
too black to be five-fifths of anything.

For more than ten scores,
as if he were the creator of all things,
the Judas of democracy kissed and betrayed us
when he said black was
three-fifths[1] of five-fifths,

two-fifths too short a human being.

And when humanity demanded democracy to
pay the weight of its hypocrisy, it kissed and
betrayed us once more
posing as the great redeemer,
amending its paper constitution as restitution
to evade taxing its cash reserves.

Two eyes, two ears, two-fifths too short,
too black to be five-fifths... *still.*
Nothing changes... nothing will.

Three fifths[1] of five-fifths,
as if it was creator of all things,
white democracy does the least of all things to
keep three-fifth[1] two-fifths too short
a human being,

the least of all things to mitigate taxation
to further its cash reserves.

♠

---
[1] United States Constitution, Article I, Section II

I've got to keep moving,
can't slow down,
I fear life will pass me by.

Too poor to sit down,
nowhere to sit.
Too black to stand still,
no place left standing
to stand on my own.

Too young to die,
not old enough to
let life pass me by.
I am running from
life and death.

So I keep moving, right to left.
My mind races ahead,
feet and body can't keep up.
They'll catch up later.
They always do, they have to,
they're too black to stand still,
got to keep moving.
Picking and weaving
in and out of cotton fields turning
into killing fields turning into cotton fields
turning back and forth again.

Got to keep moving,
heard truth and honor
made their way home safely
but I don't see them anywhere.

Read that all men were created equal,
but I can't find them anywhere,
so I keep moving.

Always climbing white mountain tops
looking to be free.

Always inquiring.

Always lifting heavy white rocks
looking for equality.

Can't slow down,
got to keep moving.

Don't want to stop asking questions.
Don't want to die without the answers.
Don't want to die under heavy white rocks.
So I keep moving.

♠

Speaking In Black

Immersed in disbelief,
he looked me in my eyes . . . surprised.

He said I did not speak in black
when we spoke on white telephones.

He said he had high hopes and opportunities
but when
he looked me in my eyes,
his eyes said pull back... backtrack,
double back and take back.

When he looked me in my eyes,
his eyes said not sounding black
is not white enough to grant access
to white hopes and opportunities.

When all that he could see in me was black,
he backtracked, doubled back,
got back in line to tow the line
and took back high hopes and opportunities
whites set aside for white.

♠

The greatest force in life
is that which asks us
to preserve ourselves,
followed closely by the fear
of not being able to do so.

It is this fear that prevents us
from living harmoniously in a
world we perceive there to be a scarcity
of valued resources to control our destiny.

It is a destructive tale and trail
of man's fears hoarding wealth and resources
repeated throughout the world in Irish
Catholics killing Irish Protestants,
Chinese killing Chinese,
Russians killing Russians,
Africans killing Africans,
Arabs killing Arabs.

A destructive tale and trail of
America establishing, not just how much of
America another American will have access to,
but how much of an American that American
will be in America.

This has been my American tale
in black and white.

White America's fears institutionalized my
black skin as an identifiable icon to exploit to
preserve their social, political and economic
gains and advantages.

As a means to secure these advantages,
white fears debased, devalued and
dehumanized Nigger as a disparaging and
degrading word to justify and verbalize my
black skin as ignorant, inferior and subhuman.

Nigger, that word which signals white America
to take legal, religious and moral leave, by any
means necessary[1], to disenfranchise black skin
as a means to ease white fears.

Nigger, that word that chews like bitter herbs
to reminds us that there has been no exodus
from this bondage.

Nigger, Brutus' dagger tip dipped in deceit and
thrust deep into the unsuspecting loins
of my being.

Nigger, that word that devalues and dehumanizes
my failures and triumphs, my joys and sorrows, my
love and losses that are the totality of my being.

Nigger, my tragic trilogy preserved and played out before a stacked white house impatiently waiting for their curtain of fear to rise before staged democracy.

♠

---
[1] *By Any Means Necessary* Speech, June 1964 by Malcolm X

Dr. Nigger

Dr. Nigger

Can you cure me without
touching me with nigga hands

Can you save my life
without changing my life

Can you dance soft-shoe while
humming those negro tunes
when my white life codes blue

Can you reach inside yourself
beyond the shit we put in you...
past painful moments we put in you...
past despair and hopelessness
we've put in you and
find that old black magic in you
to save my life without changing
all the shit we put in you

Dr. Nigger

Can you breathe in me
air free of nigga
from a nigger not free
to breathe in free air

Can you stay on the colored side
of the color line and reach across
without touching me with nigga hands
to restart my blue heart without
changing my cold heart

Can you reach past the life
we've taken from you to
save my life and not
let white life pass me by

Dr. Nigger
save my life
without taking my life

Cure me without
touching me with nigga hands

Dance soft-shoe while
humming negro tunes
while you save my life
without changing my life
when my white life codes blue

♠

9-11, 24-7

For black Americans,
9-11 is 24-7,

a labyrinth of terror buried beneath shallow
words on revised pages of America's iniquities
dating back four hundred years,
when blacks were snatched and kidnaped,
ship jacked and hijacked to America's labor and
concentration camps to be bought and sold
into unspeakable servitude on land we would
come to lose ground to some
lesser place and foreign cause.

For black Americans,
9-11 is 24-7,

... an endless cycle of America's weapons of black
destruction crashing and imploding, 24-7, into
towering black hopes and aspirations...

... a viciousness finding continuous
momentum in prescribed brutality,
administered 24-7, to infuse in us
enough terror to keep us in a lesser
place for economic gain.

For black Americans,
9-11 is 24-7,

Four hundred years and more of
democratic sleight of hands,
jiving and conniving, slipping and sliding across
smoke and mirrors...

... Jeffersonian poker face democracy
bluffing its hand of freedom,
always with the ace of tyranny
concealed up its white sleeve
to place race-based road blocks
strategically on unpaved roads to
nowhere to ensure that blacks get there...

... discriminating mercenary legislative, judicial
homicide beheading black men from the souls
of black homes and families; cutting short the
lives of one out of twenty black men
imprisoned ten times the rate of white men's
crimes[1] as a means of genteel genocide to keep
us from finding from among us a deliverer to
lead us from this lesser place...

... a good old boy network of
murder, rape and intimidation,
torture, beatings and mutilation,
social isolation and economic decimation to
keep us enslaved children of slave children
ripped from the breasts of slave mothers sold
into tortuous misery by those first families
hooded in democracy.

For black Americans,
9-11 is four hundred years and more
of America crashing and imploding,
24-7, into our towering black
hopes and aspirations.

Four hundred years and more of
no reprieves, no parity, no sign of mercy,
no justice, no relief in sight for us...

... no world coalitions proffering UN resolutions
for economic restitution...

... no international peace keepers
amassing at these plantation shores to destroy
America's weapons of mass black destruction...

... no search and rescue teams to search and
rescue us from the ruins of America's racial
injustice and exploitation...

... no gathering dignitaries to raise our tattered
black flag half-mast, found buried deep
beneath the shallow hypocrisy on revising
white pages of America's history.

... no 9-11 commission to investigate the
disposition of 36 million[2] holocaust victims
swept quietly and anonymously under white
stars and stripes forever.

... no day and time set aside to memorialize
four hundred 9-11s, each with nine thousand
black men, women and children stacked black
side up, black high to make easy America's
economic climb...

... no marked graves black with names
to fare - thee - well to distant sounds of tolling
bells...

... no heaven or hell to turn back or put back
black hopes and aspirations snatched and
kidnaped, ship jacked and hijacked.

For black Americans,
9-11 is 24-7.

♠

---

[1] Human Rights Watch - United States, *Punishment and Prejudice: Racial disparities in the War on Drugs*; www.hrw.org/campaigns/drugs/war/key-facts.htm

[2] *African American History*, Melba J. Duncan, Ch. 3, p. 31

Having been imprinted to what appeared to be, the undeniably clear and conscious importance of education, goals and perseverance, I stood like a mighty ship poised and readied before an open sea of endless possibilities, to be launched, my maiden voyage in search of new worlds.

With goals to compass me, perseverance to anchor me in turbulent seas and a learned winds blowing into full sails bellowing to capacity with longings to set a sea, I launched into the vastness of human possibilities.

Every port and shore I moored, I came to see, relative to my white colleagues, a diminished vastness in opportunities and possibilities accessible to me.

At a purely emotional glance, it appeared to be solely because I was black. A closer look revealed it was deeper than black. It was not simply because I was black.

A more critical view revealed it was because I had no wealth or valued resources to matter to those who transform their wealth and resources into power.

As such, I was no more than properly processed substrate, readied to perpetuate white exploitation for white economic gains.

I had come to realize on those distant shores that in America, a black man with no economics... they called nigger. A black man with economics... they still called nigger, but they call that nigger more frequently to participate in this illusion called the American dream. I had come to realize on distant shores that in America, formal education, perseverance and goals are fragments of pieces of the puzzle, freedom.

Formal education was not the answer. Education was not freedom. It was a means to economic ends not fully touched and tied by black hands.

It goes deeper than black.

Perseverance and goals were not the answers. They were not freedom. They were means to economic ends not fully touched and tied by black hands.

It ran deeper than black.

These fragments of pieces, in and of themselves, without economic transformation into wealth and valued resources for power, only added greater distraction and insurance that blacks stayed the means for white wealth and power.

Race, creed, color, religious indoctrination, gender, disabilities, age, formal and denied education are all discriminating tools skillfully used by the exploiters to craft, control and maintain their economic gains and advantages... ends fully tied.

I had come to realize on distant shores
that my freedom is more closely tied to economic empowerment.

It goes deeper than black.

Throughout history, it has been economic empowerment that has enslaved and freed men.

It was economics that enslaved us. Economics that allegedly emancipated us and it will be economics that will ultimately empower us to truly be free.

Wealth is and will forever be the true invulnerable earthly method by which one obtains and maintains independence and self-sustenance.

Right or wrong, like it or not, wealth and valued resources determine one's level of independence and self-emancipation.

This is not to minimize nor disregard the begrudging concessions of illusionary freedom and social gains embodied in our carefully titrated civil, voting and educational rights. They, too, are fragments of pieces of the puzzle of freedom we mistaken too often for freedom in and of themselves.

Rationed civil rights will take us but so far when affirmation and allocation of those black rights abide in the deciding white hands of uncivilized man.

Education will take us but so far when much of what we are denied and taught is intentionally calculated to misinform and miseducate to misdirect us from our economic ends.

Voting will take us but so far when candidates we have to choose from are dredged from the bottom of the pool of controllable cronies put into office through rigged elections to sell our lives and liberty to the highest corporate bidder.

These fragments of pieces served their purpose. They have begrudgingly provided small and brief windows of opportunities collectively we could have transformed into economic ends yet to be touched and tied by black hands, had we not been distracted from and unschooled of their economic ends;

had we not mistaken them for freedom in and of themselves.

Our freedom and that of our children lie in mining all our individual and collective resources to an empowering economic end to obtain true voting, civil and educational power, lest we continue to spiral short of being free.

Ours is a challenge to make ready to unite our communities and amass our collective economics, not for the sake of economics but economics for power; and power not for the sake of power, but power that empowers us to create and sustain emancipating social and political reforms receptive and responsible not only to black men, but all men.

In the struggle for freedoms in America, black men are uniquely qualified and time-tested through long suffering and deprivation to stand poised and readied to be the true founding fathers and standard bearers for all men, of freedom, liberty and justice promised, but kept from all but a few.

We must be the light where there is none; mighty ships standing poised and readied before open seas of endless possibilities launched on maiden voyages into the vastness of human possibilities.

With our individual and collective economic power, we can move mountains and build bridges of hope between human suffering and despair.

We can part the turbulent seas of social
deprivation for all to safely pass through.

So much and so many beyond us are relying on
us for freedoms and dignities promised all, but
not yet fully realized by all.

Born to this old world, I shall spend the balance
of my life, this my maiden voyage, with wind
filled sails bellowing to capacity
in search of new world
opportunities and possibilities.

I shall do so clear in purpose, certain of the way
and determined once and for all to be free and
self-sustaining.

♠

Tuskegee Air Men,
safer flying and fighting
in skies of enemy territory
than walking the streets of the country
they fought and died to defend.

♠

Straight Ahead

Straight don't have curves.
Straight can't twist or turn.

It won't look back
because it can't turn back.

Like a broken heart,
straight won't take you back.

Straight don't have twists or turns,
you can't turn back.

Straight ahead, freedom is straight
without detours, without twists or turns.
No about faces, turnabouts or curves,

freedom has but one face,
straight ahead.

♠

An effective black leader
is one who is
knowledgeable of,
but thinks and acts
outside, the white box
with clarity and conviction
and without compromise.

An effective black leader
is one who knows
that knowledge is not power.

Power is power.

But that knowledge,
tells one where best
and from which box
to wheel that power.

An effective black leader knows that
peace and freedom stand tranquil
atop the imminent threat, in their defense,
of measurable economic violence.

♠

White Snow

I am trapped on thin ice
covered in white snow.
Nowhere to step,
nowhere to go.
I have no tomorrow so
my soul howls for liberty
like swirling wintry winds
trapped down blind alleyways.

Trapped on thin ice
covered in white snow.
I have no tomorrow so
my frozen tears stare in mirrors
that won't look back;

stare in mirrors
that won't reflect black;

stare in mirrors that
I can't see myself
see myself dream
to feel my dreams
feel reality.

Strung out on thin ice
covered in white snow,
my frozen tears search
through tears
that fill the years
that fill the days that fill the tears that
mark the passing years of
unfulfilled promises.

Nowhere to step,
I look ahead in mirrors
that won't look back.
Nowhere to go,
I stare in mirrors
that won't reflect black.

Strung out covered in white snow,
freewill neither free nor within my will,
I have no more life to give.
My soul and frozen tears howl like
winter's wind trapped down blind alleyways
covered in white snow,
for freedom I will never know.

♠

In everywhere I turn,
in everywhere I reach,
in all that I see,
white faces
framed in white places
hanging on black walls
constricting time and space around me,
pushing up and down on me;
boxing me in,
to box me out
within black walls that ensure
that in every turn I turn in,
in every bend I lean in;
more turns in the turns,
more bends in the bends
pushing up and down on me.

I can't see to see
what's in front of me
when all I see is
white faces framed in white places
hanging on black walls
squeezing time and space around me;
squeezing my insides outside of me;
squeezing my dreams back up in me.

Pushing up and down on me,
inwardly spiraling my circle of being;
shrinking me until there is
nothing left of my soul and me
in every turn I turn in,
in every bend I lean in;
between blacks walls constricting
time and space around me,
that push up and down on me
with white faces framed in white places
black faces can never go.

♠

When massa's whip grew to be
in conflict with his 1776 Madison Avenue
founders of democracy ad campaign,
he conceived a new trick in subliminal
semantic culpability.

Pushing down up and pulling up down.
Flipping things all around in black men do
crimes while white men experience
momentary lapses in good judgment.

Pushing inside out and outside in.
Flipping things around in black men tell lies
and cannot be trusted while genteel white
men are less than candid for the greater
good of the nation.

It's all in what they say.

From Jefferson saying it was consensual,
Washington saying he never told a lie,
Lincoln saying he saved the day freeing black
slaves from the white man's way.

It's all in what they say.

Pushing down up and pulling up down.
Flipping things all around in blacks are drug
addicts, while whites have substance abuse
afflictions to prescriptive pain medication.

It's all in what they say.

Pushing inside out and outside in.
Flipping things around against affirmative
action to detract from white subsidies and
no bid cost plus contracts.

When massa's whip grew to be a threat to his
economic grip, he conceived a new way to
beat down black skin in subliminal semantic
culpability.

It's all in what massa says.

Surreptitiously choosing and presenting
words and ideas with titrated contrasting
amounts of subliminal blame as a means to
subconsciously diminish and devalue the
standing of one human to that of another
for inhumane economic gains.

It's all in what whites say,

In leave no tot behind,
but to hell with mom and pop;
liquor store vs wine & spirit shop,
deceiving vs spinning,
lobbying vs bribery,
colonizers vs defenders of freedoms
and liberties,
crack vs cocaine,
urban vs suburban... it's all in the name.
Jehad vs Crusades...

It's all in what whites say
in subliminal semantic culpability.

♠

Slavery,
the largest and longest
economic expansion period
for white inside trading bull markets,
still paying white preferred stockholders
above market dividends...

... still selling short,
black shares of liberty.

♠

A Nigger Can't Write a Manifesto

When America tells a nigger no,
a nigger can't write a manifesto.
A nigger can't disclaim his skin to sneak in.
A nigger can't change his name or
change his nose to avoid the obstacles
and liabilities inherent in being negro.

A nigger can't secretly drive up and
discretely leave timed pipe bombs
in white suburban mail boxes without
the likelihood of being detained for
unlawfully driving while black, in a white
neighborhood redlined to be black free.

A nigger ain't allowed to drive white free,
when America tells a nigger no.

Negroes aren't allowed to come and go as
they please. Niggers aren't allowed to
wander white free.

A nigger can't brutalize his wife at morning's
light, dispose of her bludgeoned body by noon,
and lead the national prayer and search for her
decaying corpse by the close of that same day.

Niggers aren't allowed to blow when
dreams don't become reality.

Niggers aren't allowed to go off, white free.

When America tells a nigger no,
a nigger can't write a manifesto.

Niggers can't brazenly walk into a flight school
flashing cash in return for lessons flying a plane
while dispensing with taking off and landing.

Niggers aren't allowed to fly with deficiencies.
Niggers raise questions flashing cash to fly,
white free.

Niggers can't run Enron like Enron ran end runs
around stockholders and government regulators.

Niggers can't run around as they please.
Niggers aren't allowed to run, white free.

A nigger takes the complete fall for all the
drugs on America's streets despite the fact
niggers don't have the financial and
distributional capabilities to traffic drugs into
America because niggers aren't allowed
white liberties.

A nigger can't evade and delay jail time with insincere apologies and remorsing to cue for pay for view and made for prime time TV.

Niggers don't get air time, niggers get time. Niggers get time, but niggers can't change the times because a nigger can't nominate and vote his candidate when bona fide black nominees are marginalized to the radical fringes in the confusion of making too much sense; or dismissed in America's stand by manifesto that Americans are not yet ready for a nigger president.

Niggers aren't allowed to represent.
Niggers aren't allowed to run white free.
A nigger can't write a manifesto to tell America no when America tells him to forfeit his one vote in choosing between the lesser of two white nominees or, black faced puppets, whites stand behind with their white gloved hands shoved en masse up their puppets' asses.

A nigger ain't allowed to represent.
A nigger ain't allowed to run ass hole free.

When America tells a nigger no,
a nigger can't write a manifesto.
A nigger can't lighten his skin to sneak in.
A nigger can't change his name
or change his nose to avoid the obstacles
and liabilities inherent in being negro.

A nigger can't write a manifesto,
when America tells a nigger no.

♠

Between Soiled Sheets

"By the dawn's early light[1],
the founding fathers of freedom and
democracy found their way to rape the
mothers of my mother.

At twilight's last gleaming
there, *on the shore dimly seen*
thro' the mists of the deep[1]

they raped our shackled black mothers
between kneeling and praying
to that white Jesus the white man
sold them would come
to save them from him...

... raped our slaved mothers
between pleading and screaming,
between screaming and weeping,
between weeping and whimpering
between the soiled sheets of
freedom and democracy.

Raped, one at a time,
time after time until the distant moon
reflecting in their detached silent gazes
turned away to shed tears as founding
fathers of liberty undressed the mothers of
my mother one at a time, time after time,
between the soiled sheets
of freedom and democracy.

Between their rockets' red glare,
and bombs bursting in air[1]
there, between the soiled sheets
of freedom and democracy,
the founding fathers of liberty
raped our mothers until their defiant curly
hairs acquiesced and fell limp down, across
their undressed shoulders.

Raped until our slave mothers'
black skin bred and bled
laddered mulattos caste[d] by hue,
to pave the road to our despair,
our affliction with self-hate, our addiction to
dependency and division.

Raped until our slave mothers'
black skin bred and bled
our identity in white things
and white dreams.

There beneath that
star-spangled banner yet wav[ing] [1]
the founding fathers of liberty
raped us of our mothers' dreams,
our fathers' history,
our human dignity,
our methods and means,
our manhood, our selfhood,
the legacy handed to legacies,
there, between those soiled sheets of
star-spangled freedom and democracy.

♠

---
[1] *Star Spangled Banner* by Francis Scott Key, 9.14.1814

Past

Clock hands move but
time still stands still.

Encased and cast in constant
emerging emergence,
the past is in today still.

Time stands still as
clock hands move in circles
back to around again.

Future is forecast in that
circular past that keeps passing back and
forth in front of me,
reminding me in pendular passes
my future is the past with me,
pacing back and forth in me.

My future is this use to be,
that still is.
That outlook looking back,
this emeritus that keeps
working amongst us facing me,
hoping me, pacing me back and forth in me,
reminding me in its ceaseless passing
my past is in today still.

♠

Give to Get

Because we fear the threat of hell
far more than the rebuff of heaven,
we seek forgiveness without repentance.

We enslave then seek
forgiveness to enslave again.
We kill then seek
forgiveness to kill again.

We don't give to give,
we give to get without repentance
because we fear the thought of hell
more than the loss of heaven.

We give, not that others may be healed and
delivered, we give to receive healings and
deliverance for ourselves.

We give to have the seeds we've sowed
return back, twenty fold.

We let go so we can hold tightly,
piousness in one hand
and righteousness in the other,

Like shield and sword drawn not
in quest of the promise land but
in defense against the threat of hell.

Because we fear the threat of hell
we hedge our bet without regrets
and seek forgiveness without repentance.

We hate then seek
forgiveness to hate again.
We destroy then seek
forgiveness to destroy again.
We take then seek
forgiveness to take again.

We don't do right to be Christlike,
we pretend to do right to get
everlasting life.

We deceive to make others believe
we sincerely give to give, but in
reality we hedge the bet and give to get
to repel our fears of hell's threat.

♠

The Look of Freedom

I am convinced
that for black Americans,
the look of freedom
has been more detrimental
than no freedom at all.

I am convinced we have long since
delayed real freedom for
the look of freedom and in the process, have lost
our ability to distinguish
between the two.

I am convinced that for black Americans,
perceived integration has succeeded
in segregating us not only from ourselves
but from churning black dollars into
black financial backbones and
wealth building stepping stones
into and through mainstream American.

We have traded black economic integration for
financial segregation, subordination and
domination of black haves and black have nots.

We have traded black economic integration for
financial segregation and alienation of black
haves from the blacker have nots.

Divided and distinguishable, we have
sold our individual birthrights for
consumer rights to buy white,
to look more white,
to look like we are indistinguishably white
and in the process
we have lost our ability to distinguish real
freedom from the look of freedom.

I am convinced
that for black Americans,
the look of freedom
has been more detrimental
than no freedom at all.

♠

With hair like wool and feet as black as burnt brass[1], he would have been asked to read the signs that told negroes to stand in the line - For Colored People Only.

With hair like wool and feet as black as burnt brass[1], he would have been asked to disembark or march his dark ass right back to the back, alongside Rosa Park.

Beset in a Woolworth luncheonette, he would have sat and been denied food service alongside four silhouettes of the Greensboro quartet; despite having walked on water[2] he turned to wine[3] and transforming five loaves of bread and bits of sun dried fish to bounty to feed the needs of ten scores times twenty[4].

He would have been fire blown from house and home, stoned and water hosed by robed men posing as disciples.

Hit at and bit at, spit at by bureaucrats, aristocrats and proletariats masquerading as diplomats of democracy, he would have been made to fear hell rising from the very cross man's redemption hung on as it set a blazed, hooded in suspended darkness to impart terror in him.

With hair like wool and feet as black as burnt
brass[1], he would have walked the path of
Abraham to march in mass from Selma to
Montgomery, to be knocked down, to be nailed
down, to be held down jailed down in
Birmingham to rise again to march again with
Martin on to Washington.

Onward through gridlock streets
of scorn and thorns, to mountain
tops where dreams are sought.

To Mount Sinai, to Mount Look Out in route
to Stone Mountain rooftops, where men are
shot spreading dreams of democracy
too evenly down serpentine streets
divided unevenly by white lines.

On to Calvary he would have walked, steadfast
through the hour's last passing through the
narrowed path in the hour's glass for hair like
wool and feet as black as burnt brass[1].

Steadfast through unremitting brutality.

Steadfast being told to hell with negro
redemption, to lay his black ass across the cross
and bleed...

there are no line items nor need
for salvation across the white pages of
profit and loss sheets...

silver and gold hold more esteem...

that assets mean more to tyranny than a prophet
featured with hair like wool and feet as black as
burnt brass[1], thought not to be worthy the savior
of humanity.

♠

---
[1] Revelations 1, 14, 15
[2] John 6, 16-21
[3] John 2, 3-10
[4] Matthew 14, 13-21

Ray

Having never seen
purple mountain majesties[1]
except as perceived in dreams
seen in his own mind's eye,
Ray Charles sang America The Beautiful
with such grace and dignity.

Had he eyes to see
what eyes would see
if eyes could see
from sea to shining sea[1]
he would have seen with much
less grace and dignity...

no black spacious skies,
and amber waves of grain,
no purple mountain majesties
above fruited plain[s][1]...

no black patriot dream
that sees beyond the years
thine alabaster cities gleam
undimmed by human tears[1]...

no black pilgrim feet
whose stern impassioned stress
a thoroughfare of freedom beat
across this wilderness[1]...

no black [glory-tale of liberating strife
when once and twice,
for *white*[2] man's avail, *white*[2] men lavished
precious life] [1] expensed
in black cash and sacrifice.

Had he eyes to see
what eyes would see
if eyes could see
from sea to shining sea[1],
he would have sung
America The Beautiful
with lesser grace and dignity to
plead God shed no grace on thee
until thee mend thine every flaw,
confirm thy soul in self-control,
thy liberty[1] *in impartial*[2] law[1]...

until, thy gold refine... till all success be
nobleness and every gain[1], *a selfless gain that
taints and stains no longer more
that tattered*[2] *banner of the free*[1]...

... till nobler men keep once again thy whiter jubilee[1] *white free*[2] through amber waves of grain and purple mountain majesties above fruited plain[s][1] *that span for every man that perceives and sees*[2] *from* sea to shining sea[1].

♠

---
[1] *America The Beautiful* by Katherine Lee Bates
[2] Author's added or amended text

N-Word

The N-word,

a nigga laced Trojan horse construct for nigger
assembled in apparent white concede in the
wake of white retreat,

left outside the fortified walls of militarized
consciousness in hollowed tribute to a
mendacious victory over white
siege and tyranny.

... a luring steed, left as inconspicuous evidence
of massa's insincere sensibilities
to our nigger sensitivities...

... a statuesque stallion lair, pushed and pulled
in the revel of revelry passed fortified gates of
demilitarized consciousness, to lie in wait for
time and place to disembowel its nigger snare.

The N-word,
mo mutating white phraseology
evolving politically correct from its primeval
ancestry – jig a boo, jungle bunny, darkie,
monkey, tar baby, Nigger, Nigga, Negro, African,
Afro-American, African American, black.

... mo white phraseology evidencing
massa's evolving insincere sensibilities
to our nigger sensitivities.

Mo white phraseology lying in nigger wait for
time and place beneath white whispers, behind
black backs...

... when the camera fades black and
the sound turns down... when nigga skin buys
next door before whites have a chance to move
away before nigga skin moves in next door...

... in war rooms and board rooms of
country clubs, where generals plot their
next socioeconomic offense...

... when affirmative action sips from the
fountain of white privilege and patronage.

N-word... mo white treachery in phraseology
lying in nigger wait for time and place to
disembowel their nigger snare.

♠

Six Letters Away

I am six letters away from a downhill slide
on the slippery side of an uphill climb.

Six letters away from never ever being
able to sever myself from never ever.

Six letters away from being backspaced
to be disgraced, to be misplaced, to be
displaced back into my proper place.

Six letters away from never ever being
severed from never ever.

I am only six letters away from being slain
openly high on a mountain top of blood stained
spots dripping down continuously from the
balcony of Hotel Lorraine.

Six letters away from one red neck bullet
spun from a Bryon De Beckwith gun.

Six letters away from being beaten,
mutilated and tossed into a raging Tallahatchie
River to remind me that never means forever.

Six letters away from decapitation while
being detained and restrained by chains tied to
the back end of pick up trucks for black men.

Six letters away from never ever being severed from six letters spewed in my face to let me know that wherever I go, whatever station I hold, my defined place is only six letters away from a downhill slide on the slippery side of the uphill climb of never ever.

♠

Citadel

Disheartened citadel,
paladin of the inalienable,
spiraling down this one-way stairwell,

lost its way to heaven
on this man-made road to
handmade hell.

Spent lifetimes to find
I have run out of life and time,
black and blue colliding on the
inside of black and bruised.
I give up... gave out.

Disheartened citadel,
expending my life to find
only loss of life and time
which gave up.

I fell in,
ran out of knees to pray on,
beliefs to stand on.

Long past the cry in me,
what used to be
I gave up,
fell in,
ran out,
gave up to give up
spending life and time spiraling
black and blue,
black and bruised
down this man-made road to
handmade hell.

♠

Preoccupation with occupation...
... there is a life and poem in there.

Whiteness prevents alabaster skin...
... there is a poem in there seeing out as
fellow human being.

My bloody colored skin...
... there is life in there,
pleading out as fellow human being,
"there is a life in there".

Crying out at fellow human beings,
I am a poem in here,
there is a life somewhere in
uncharacteristic hell telling not so
my distilled contempt of
nature's stall to call not,
my bloody color skin
and tragic heart,
to dilute my passion of it.

What is there in it in there
striving to be free within captivity.

There is life and poem in there,
there is a life and poem in there.

♠

Of Freedom

Like Charlie Bird and Baldwin
Prince and Count Basie
Dionne Warwick and Savion

Like Jack Johnson and Gillespie
Ray and Sugar Ray

Like earth, the wind and fire

Like Nas and Topac

Like Chris Rock's
antidotal anecdotes

Ella skipping, scatting
between melodized notes

Like Ali and Socrates
Aretha and Miles Davis
Coltrane and Sade

Like
Malcolm X and Cornel West,
this subtle, fleeting, easing
of shackles squeezed
about wrist, to feel
in finger tips
this faint textured sense...
of freedom

♠

Choice?

Nowhere
in the threat of hell
is,
free choice.

Nowhere
in no choice
is,
free choice.

Nowhere
in the threat of hell,
is there
a choice of free will nor
a free choice for eternal life.

♠

Heralded Strategies

Heralded strategies,
misguided and oversold,
mistakenly held by blacks
as a way of life for life.

Nonsecular brews
churning in caldrons,
turning inebriated lions
into passive sheep
to graze nonviolently,

to march in turn, peacefully
greeting brutality turning
tongues and cheeks.

Heralded strategies,
diminishing, limiting our thinking
and reactions to diminishing and limiting
life and liberty to a standard well below
by any means necessary[1].

Unwise to narrow the discourse.
Misguided to limit the battle's course.

Turn back history's pages to see
their founding fathers found
means and necessity
to turn back to shoot back
colonizing red coats
diminishing, limiting their
life and liberty.

♠

---
[1] *By Any Means Necessary,* Speech by Malcolm X, June 1964

Hope and Rescue

There is no shepherd
to put eyes upon the watch
of lamb and sheep
led to graze in withered pastures
gnawed of hope and rescue.

There is no second coming.
No divine being to put eyes
upon the watch of discriminating wolves
circling, openly shearing flesh and bone
from flesh and bone;
ripping life and breath from suckled breast;
viciously slaughtering lambs and sheep
beyond the canine's need;
beyond white hunger's need to eat.

There is no shepherd
to put eyes upon this watch.
There is but lamb and sheep,
led away like lamb and sheep
to graze before wolves
in withered pastures gnawed
of hope and rescue.

♠

This We Wear

This, we wear as freedom.
This odorous secondhand garment
tattered and ragged,
dipped in blood,
drenched in brethren's woes
and rigor mortis.

This, we wear as freedom,
as if real this independence,
as if evidence of redemptive parity,
as if born of battles of hearts and minds won.

Crumbling crumbs of contaminated equality,
picked over scraps,
fetid morsels of liberty
lobbed casually from passing callousness
to fall foul on drenched feet standing yet
held bondage still in their brethren's
woes and rigor mortis.

This, we see as freedom.
This, we wear as freedom,
as if real,
this facsimile of blackened independence.

♠

Mottos of Hypocrisy

Forward,
Ready in mind and resources
We dare defend our rights
To be rather than to seem.

Wisconsin, South Carolina
Alabama, North Carolina

Our liberties we prize and
our rights we will maintain.
By Valor and Arms
By the sword we seek peace
but peace under liberty.

Iowa, Mississippi,
Massachusetts

United we stand, divided we fall
Liberty and union now and forever,
one and inseparable
It grows as it goes
Ever upward.

Kentucky, North Dakota
New Mexico, New York

While I breathe, I hope
Freedom and unity
Virtue, liberty and independence
Equal rights
Justice for all.

South Carolina, Vermont
Pennsylvania, Wyoming, DC

The welfare of the people shall be
the highest law.
Thus always to tyrants.

Missouri, Virginia

♠

And God Said

The lighter man said,
And God said,
let there be white.

Creation and Creator,
recreated to enrich lighter skin.
Turned Genesis inside out
to keep darker skin from getting in.
Revisionists, reinventing Genesis
to say, And God said.

Contortionist, twisting Genesis
to lay claim
the lighter man said,
And God said
HE divided light from dark.

He said the God of everything
said HE created him,
not me in HIS holy likeness.

The revisionists revised Genesis and said,
And God said lighter skin
shall hold dominion over fish
and fowl and all the earth and
every creeping thing that creeps there[1].

Turned Genesis inside out.

The white man laid low six feet,
blackness, to creep and crawl
on servant knees to have dominion over
and in the end said,

God said.

♠

---
[1] Genesis 1: 26

Urban Slave Ships

Urban slave ships rushing
to and fro new world destinations.

Four-wheel all terrain slave ships
token(ed) and timed,
loading and unloading queued up
sunrise(d) negro cargo
destined for suburban paradise.

Urban buses,
shuttling and shuffling
to and fro;
importing, exporting
expendable negro cargo
between sunrise, sunset;
between suburban malls, urban ghettos.

Approved "busing" addressing suburbia's
need for negro cargo; cheap labor at
urban compensations.

We roll like that for New World
greed and exploitation.

♠

It Don't Stop

The game don't stop.
They say it do, but it don't.

It spins around spin,
eating beyond the meal,
taking beyond the reach,
killing beyond death,
changing to changing lies
drawn from a pot of props
cut and pasted into half-truths
to keep the wheel of fortune spinning,
twisting into hurricane waters rising up
to spent niggers floating face down
atop the spin.

The game don't stop.
They say it do, but it don't.

♠

Nigger Intelligencia

Seasons of unseasoned paradigms pressing back and forth unseasoned reasoning locked inside an existentialist matrix of round rooms filled with vying prophetic protagonists pressing each other round and round the intellectual room, past the gloom of uprooted wintered bloom waiting disenfranchised waste side; unable to decide through their wintered view what you are in your insides, inside the hour of your minute hands held out for a second.

Locked inside vacuous vacuoles of pretentious intellect, the real of life yet to bloom in life and room filled with the melodic cadence of chimed word chords timed to fill time to impress as they press back and forth out of tune, out of touch of outer worlds outside their round perverse pleonastic room.

♠

True Savior

I have lived long enough in this world to
realize that the best life has to offer
is that you live long enough in this world
to realize that death is the one true savior,
the dark prince of peace that is my eternal
salvation from life in this world.

♠

Democracy

Do ragged
sagging pants,
hooded out hanging out
on the corner of hypocrisy and deceit,
tucked between the narrow streets of
Justice and Liberty.

Nodding white knight
wearing cowboy black
beneath white hats,
pimping the pimps
macking the macks
bitch smacking lady liberty
as he staggers back leaning back
snorting hits
holding dick
talking shit
dealing hits
selling high hope dope
to keep black folk
strung out, high
on false hope.

♠

Footnote

Note of lesser note,
footed there at the foot
of paginated white space,

relegated to smaller print,
lesser texts
held straight in
long black lines under pretext
of lesser content and contexts,

repressed, to refer back up to
while
being referred down to
by that bigger,
bolder pretense of larger
texts, content
and contexts.

♠

Clockwise

We are surreptitiously educated and
socialized to process and think
in prescribed logic that
quickly takes leave
of perceived illogic.

It is in this preconditioning
counterclockwise clockwork orange
perceptual deceit,
the exploiter exploits,
the subjugator subjugates,
the oppressor presses on clockwise
so steeply cloaked in apparent illogic
and counterintuitive countermoves
that the most scholarly skeptics
think it so far-fetched he takes his leave,
dismissing culprit and culpability,
conspirator and conspiracy,
leaving oppressor to press on
pulling counterclockwise wool over
eyes and minds.

♠

Breakdown

Can't break me down
with your meltdowns,
breakdowns.

I am not bending,
not breaking down,
won't go down.

I am not breaking down to down,
not going to crawl there down
in your meltdowns and breakdowns.

♠

Said If I

Took youthful look
from distant star
at half-moon
said would be full.

Said if I would fly
there'd be angel wings to carry me
beyond the blue to that distant star.

Said if I would measure the reach,
take leap and faith at promised dreams
I would just fly.

Leaped,
did not measure up
as I looked up
falling back down.

Did not know there were no carrying wings
nor winds to blow above
blue skies and over rainbows
through white lies.

Did not know,
I needed to know
how to measure unknown.

Fell short,
leaping colored rainbows
hung on crossing lies
while looking at
while falling back
while reaching at half-moon
they said would soon be full
if I would just fly.

♠

Been to the mountain top
where they had me
when they asked me
to ask not,
what my country could do for me
rather, what I could do for my country[1]
whilst my country was doing me.

I've been to the mountain top,
ain't nothing there but a straight drop.
From the hilltops of New Hampshire
to the Alleghenies of Pennsylvania,
from the snowcapped Rockies
to the slopes of California[2],
there ain't no kings
no promised land
no embracing hands.

Ain't no freedom's ring,
no we in We The People.
My eyes can't see anything
but dated niggers clinging
to a nightmare posing as their dream.
Can't free nobody if your mind ain't free
to see the song won't sing

[Our] county tis of thee;
sweet land of liberty...
Land where [our] fathers died...
from every mountain [top]
let freedom ring[3].

I've been to that mountain top,
ain't nothing there but a straight drop.

♠

---
[1] John F. Kennedy's Inaugural Address, 1.20.61
[2] *I Have a Dream*, Speech, Martin Luther King, 8.28.63
[3] *America, (My Country This of Thee)*, S. F. Smith, 1831

High Mentality

gots high mentality.

a high yella thin skin state of mind
a few hues removed from that
one drop makes a nigger theory.

a little less black to be
a little less nigga
the color black can be.

high yella mentality,

yellow fevered delusions of perceived freed
men cause you sit in massa's house,
protects his shit whilst massa lynch
mo field niggas.

gots urine stained emancipation,
validation 'cause you gets to guard
massa's shit,
holding it as if you owned it,
holding it whilst massa
poke mo field niggas with massa's dick.

gots you housed in the house blue suit,
cotton white shirt, a yella ring about your collar,
content, crouching in corporate cotton fields,
holding up glass ceilings with the crown of your
yella state of mind.

gots mo pride holding and beholden
than being black and free.
thinks yous not a nigga,
cause you thinks niggas don't get to
hold massa's shit,
wear massa's shit
whilst massa pokes mo field niggas
with massa's dick.

gots a wide yellow streak
wedged in the crack between
both halves of your black ass.

yous in a high yella state of mind,
a high mentality away from the reality
one drop makes a nigga theory.

gots to be a little less black to be
a little less nigga
the color black can be.

♠

Property

Mother's frantic cries,
try,
fall shy,
muted,
by the rising clangs of her panic struck slave
chains,
reaching,
pulling,
tearing at
my chattel remains reaching back,
pulling at,
tearing at
her watery womb
as the slaver
reaches my way,
pulling me away from
mother's frantic tries
as she cries
above the rising clangs of her panic struck
slave chains.

♠

Like Mine

To see their tears,
why must eyes look like mine?

To feel their pain,
why must eyes cry like mine?

How do you walk away?
How do we say this be not my tear,
this, not my pain?

Is not wind, wind whether
North, East, South or West?

When brown is not blue,
the blue not brown,
what do we tell same hearts to be,
in order to be heartless to sound
of tear from eyes that are not
like mine?

♠

Epilogue

Written in black and white, this is
a revealing look inside an awakening
mind reflecting and speaking to itself
as it painfully gives birth to full
consciousness of what really is.

Written in white on black, this is
a trail of injustice any man anywhere can
inflict on any man.

To see only black and white
is to miss the slave trail,
to miss the tale of injustice.

To see just black and white
is to want to need to see only black and white
as a means to steer clear this trail
to deny seeing,
to deny being the injustice
one man has and continues to inflict
upon another man.

To see only black and white
is to miss seeing
what any man anywhere
can inflict on any man
as revealed in the injustice
the white man has and
continues to inflict
upon the black man.

♠

Index

1776 Declaration of Independence: 1st Draft	1
9-11, 24-7	182
A kindling crowd is just a hang man's noose	149
A man can only have two masters	102
A Nigger Can't Write a Manifesto	204
A Voice	8
All in One	68
Always Some	29
An effective black leader	195
And God Said	238
Are we humans	97
Are we not prisoners of ourselves	84
Article I, Section II	172
Attitude, Aptitude, Altitude	77
Be not deceived by people	39
Because I see what eyes cannot see	93
Becoming	109
Been to the mountain top	250
Benjamins	142
Better Served	132
Between Soiled Sheets	208
Black man's lips	30
Breakdown	247
By Reason of Blackness	158
Casting	24
Choice?	231
Citadel	226
Civil Men Do	18
Clockwise	246

Collateral Benefits	82
Color	38
Democracy	244
Despite your expectations of me	90
Diallo	7
Diversification	51
Drawn within the tautness	17
Dr. Nigger	180
Epilogue	255
Equal heights	27
Even though	12
Everybody is in bed with somebody	63
Father forgive them not	59
First and Foremost	129
First Served	20
First to Die	166
Folks	140
Follower	67
Footnote	245
For a totalitarian government2	4
Freedom and dignity are like	113
Freedom is a limited commodity	116
Freedom is determined in part by the	128
Freedom Lost	117
Friendly Mr. white man	157
Give to Get	212
Grass Roots	36
Great men change bad laws	112
Great men say nothing	96
Having been imprinted to what appeared to	186
He that hears with his eyes...	114

Hence Forward	101
Heralded Strategies	232
High Mentality	252
Hope and Rescue	234
I'm a good little Negro	86
I's Free	150
I've got to keep moving	174
I've learned to what extent people will go	100
I am not brave	144
I am under no illusions	13
I can give no more time	168
I Don't Hang	138
I have found within me that anger	119
If we would rely more on the experiences	130
In America	40
In an attempt to protect ourselves	49
In art	26
In Black and White	22
In everywhere I turn	198
In front of you	37
In saying and doing nothing	5
In the Land of	74
In There	146
Inner Light	89
It	11
It Don't Stop	241
It is life's contradictions tainted with hypocrisy	16
It is the nature of humans	91
Just when I believe I am about	106
Knowing What I Be Knowing	160
Liberty is a chalice few men hold	41

Lie unmoved against me	110
Life is not enough	143
Like Mine	255
Love and hate are created equally	14
Marcus Garvey was not racist nor racism	147
Martin Luther King's birthday	28
Massa put brands on us to put discernable	164
Mohammad Ali	141
More Deception Than Reparation	162
Mottos of Hypocrisy	236
N-Word	222
Need to be in a place	98
Neutralize	70
Nigger For Life	152
Nigger Intelligencia	242
Niggers are not born	6
No Faith in Faith	94
No shore for refuge	45
Of Freedom	229
Outside Inside of Outside	154
Overcoming the fear of	103
Paradox	104
Past	211
Patronization	133
People love winning.	52
Politically speaking	42
Politicians can't get anything done	65
Prayer of Exodus	169
Preoccupation with occupation...	228
Pretense and Pretext	3
Profiling	56

Progress	21
Property	254
Purpose	88
Racial injustice and intolerance	79
Racial tension simmers	31
Ray	219
Religion	47
Said If I	248
Signature Blend	165
Sisters Say	76
Six Letters Away	224
Slavery	203
Some men see soaring birds	87
Speaking In Black	176
Standing	80
Straight Ahead	194
Surrounding myself in isolation	115
Telltale Air	156
The black man wraps himself in a flag hoist	73
The Declaration and Constitution placed	50
The evolution of freedom for all men	127
The greatest force in life	177
The Greatest of These	48
The Last of What's Left	62
The Look of Freedom	214
The majority of White Americans	25
The Point	23
The world's natural course is weighted	54
The world would be better off if Jesus	135
There are black people	81
There are those who lead men in prayer	46

There is	15
There is a truth	92
There is always a ray	148
There is no evil	53
This We Wear	235
Through institutionalized misinformation	71
To provide for America's national interest	83
True greatness	131
True Multiculturalism	32
True Savior	243
Truth is	9
Trying to be a black man in America	78
Tuskegee Air Men	193
Unto Moses, the purist of heart	122
Urban Slave Ships	240
We all are prostitutes of some sort	43
We are	58
We are conduits of	19
We are socialized and emotionalized	126
We continue futile efforts to persuade	120
We don't all need to be the same color	118
We don't have enough freedom	99
We either have no dreams	10
We must transform and transfix	134
We The People	167
Webster defines entrepreneurship	123
Weeds and Hate	55
Welcomed change must always pass	111
What People Do	136
When black people do wrong	66
When massa's whip grew to be	200

When people are too outwardly loud	108
While I realize that we all cannot	121
While we have been chasing	60
White America wants me to believe	72
White Man Asked Me	44
White people ask for patience	107
White people will only do right	64
White righteousness is	69
White Snow	196
With hair like wool and feet as black as burnt	216
You can rise up	61
You People	137